MW00573252

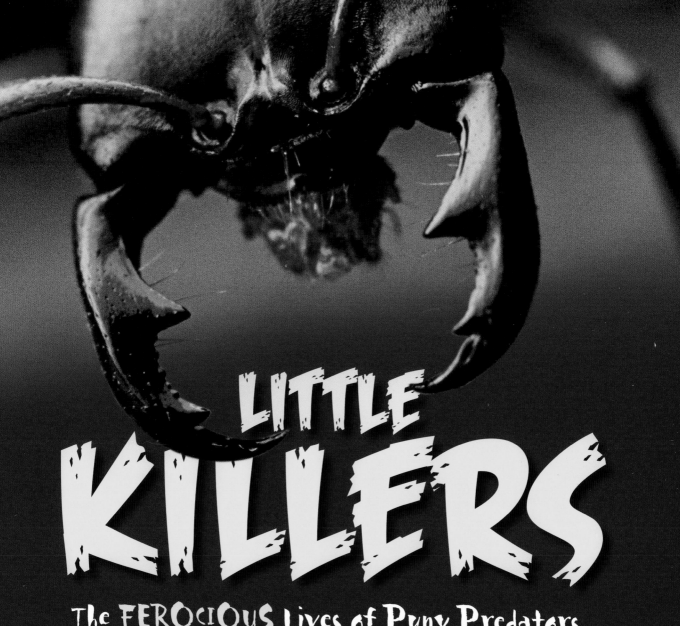

LITTLE KILLERS

The FEROCIOUS Lives of Puny Predators

Sneed B. Collard III

Ⓜ Millbrook Press / Minneapolis

To Roland and Marie Smith. Always helpful, always passionate, always friends.

Millbrook Press™
An imprint of Lerner Publishing Group, Inc.
241 First Avenue North
Minneapolis, MN 55401 USA

For reading levels and more information, look up this title at www.lernerbooks.com.

Designed by Kimberly Morales.
Main body text set in Felbridge Std.
Typeface provided by Monotype Typography.

Library of Congress Cataloging-in-Publication Data

Names: Collard, Sneed B., author.
Title: Little killers : the ferocious lives of puny predators / Sneed B. Collard III.
Description: Minneapolis : Millbrook Press, [2022] | Includes bibliographical references and index. | Audience: Ages 8–12 | Audience: Grades 4–6 | Summary: "Meet some of the world's most impressive predators! Small creatures can make a huge impact, changing ecosystems, controlling pests, and even taking down much larger creatures. Discover the amazing lives of these voracious killers" —Provided by publisher.
Identifiers: LCCN 2021011557 (print) | LCCN 2021011558 (ebook) | ISBN 9781728415697 (library binding) | ISBN 9781728445397 (ebook)
Subjects: LCSH: Predatory animals—Juvenile literature. | Parasitology—Juvenile literature.
Classification: LCC QL758 .C665 2022 (print) | LCC QL758 (ebook) | DDC 591.5/3—dc23

LC record available at https://lccn.loc.gov/2021011557
LC ebook record available at https://lccn.loc.gov/2021011558

Manufactured in the United States of America
1-48685-49103-9/13/2021

CONTENTS

CHAPTER 1
KILLERS AROUND US

A group of microscopic copepods

F ar from land, hundreds of feet below the ocean surface, a copepod (KOH-peh-pod) swims through dim, twilight waters. The copepod measures only a tenth of an inch (2.5 mm) but has two ridiculously long antennae sweeping out from its head. The animal uses its antennae to locate microscopic plants called phytoplankton. Like a contented cow, the copepod grazes on one tiny plant after another. All seems peaceful until . . .

in darts a nightmare out of a science fiction movie! The sudden arrival looks like a slim, transparent torpedo. Instead of a face, it has a menacing mouth surrounded by a nest of grasping hooks, or spines. It has stubby horizontal fins and a fanlike tail, and by wriggling up and down, it can accelerate to terrifying speeds. Faster than you can shout "free food!" the tiny torpedo seizes the copepod with its hooks and opens its mouth wide. The copepod struggles to get away, but it is no use. In an instant, the predator swallows the copepod whole.

ALARMING ARROWS

The torpedo-shaped animal is a chaetognath (KEE-tug-nath), or arrow worm. Most people have never heard of chaetognaths, but they are among Earth's most ferocious predators. Most chaetognaths live in the upper layers of the world's oceans, and most are *planktonic*—they are carried from place to place by ocean currents. Chaetognaths, though, can also live in tide pools, on the seafloor, and in the very deep sea.

THE WORD CHAETOGNATH IS LATIN FOR "BRISTLE-JAWED."

An arrow worm (*right*) uses darting speed and grasping hooks to seize tiny fish and other prey.

Hangin' Out

Chaetognaths spend a lot of time hanging suspended in the water. Their horizontal fins help keep them from sinking very rapidly. When they do sink—or detect prey—they dart forward using rapid muscle contractions in their bodies.

Chaetognaths have superb tools to help them ambush and seize their prey. Their bodies are see-through, making them almost impossible to spot, especially in the dim regions where they prefer to hunt. Tiny hairs on their skin help them detect the smallest water movements, allowing them to target their prey. Perhaps most impressive are the chaetognath's mouthparts. Hooks, or spines, surround the mouth and are used for grasping prey, while needle-sharp teeth inside its mouth help the animal pierce and swallow prey. Many chaetognaths can even inject poison into their victims!

An arrow worm's see-through body and slim profile help it sneak up on prey and escape the notice of other predators.

Chaetognaths first appeared on Earth at least five hundred million years ago. Since then, their bodies have changed very little—a sign that they are very well adapted to living where and how they do. Because of this, scientists consider them one of Earth's most successful predators. But chaetognaths also are some of Earth's *smallest* predators. While a few deep-water species can grow to 4 or 5 inches (10 to 12 cm) long, most are shorter than a pencil eraser. Chaetognaths, however, are far from Earth's only puny-sized predators.

Fisherman's Foe?

Besides eating copepods, chaetognaths are major predators of small fish and fish larvae. They may even control or limit some fish populations around the world.

TINY KILLERS

When most of us hear the word *predator*, we imagine lions sneaking through tall grass after zebras or great white sharks tearing seals to shreds. That's no surprise. Large predators—from wolves to polar bears to orcas—are some of Earth's most impressive animals. But the vast majority of Earth's predators aren't humongous lion- or whale-sized creatures. Many, such as spiders and ladybird beetles, are so small that you can easily overlook them while taking your dog for a walk. Others, such as chaetognaths, are so little you often need a microscope to see them.

SOME CHAETOGNATHS CAN EAT UP TO A THIRD OF THEIR WEIGHT EACH DAY!

What makes these little killers so successful?

MICRO-ADVANTAGES

Like larger predators, small predators come equipped with an arsenal of weapons to help them catch and subdue their prey. These weapons—such as the teeth, hooks, and transparent body of a chaetognath—are perfectly adapted to each predator's size, habitat, and way of life. Little killers also have a couple of advantages over other predators.

While a sample of creek water might look clear or empty, it may contain thousands of living organisms, including a host of tiny predators.

Mood Lighting

Scientists have discovered two species of arrow worms that are bioluminescent—they make their own light. When a predator approaches, the arrow worms release a spray of light-producing chemicals behind them, confusing the predator and allowing the arrow worms to get away.

One is that small predators have a lot more places to live. The world is only big enough to hold a limited number of lions, sharks, and wolves, but almost unlimited spaces exist for their tinier counterparts. Small predators can live in cracks, between sand grains, in muddy sediments, on leaves and flowers—and even on other, larger animals! Predators can live in so many places that scientists haven't come close to identifying all of the different kinds of little predators on our planet.

A second great advantage for puny predators is the abundance of prey. For every small predator, there may be hundreds or thousands of other miniscule animals to eat. If you search a flower bed, you might find thousands of aphids for every ladybird beetle that you see. In one Egyptian lake, scientists counted more than 120 copepods in each gallon (3.8 L) of water. With odds like these, is it any wonder that thousands—perhaps millions—of kinds of tiny predators populate our planet?

Let's turn the page and eat—I mean meet—some more of them, starting with some of the smallest.

CHAPTER 2
MICROSCOPIC MEAT EATERS

A microscopic image of a typical *Campanella*

It's a nice day in the pond, and a microscopic creature called *Campanella* is hanging around eating algae. *Campanella* is not a plant or animal but is a kind of "in between" organism, a ciliate (SIL-ee-ate). Its body is attached to an underwater plant by a thin stalk. Tiny, hairlike cilia around *Campanella*'s mouth beat back and forth, creating little water currents that sweep algae and other food toward it.

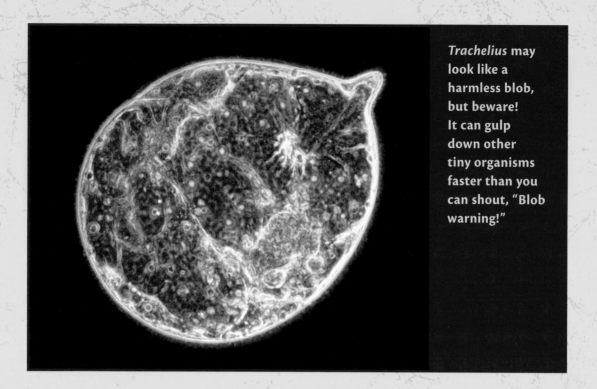

Trachelius may look like a harmless blob, but beware! It can gulp down other tiny organisms faster than you can shout, "Blob warning!"

Nearby is *Trachelius* (tra-KEE-lee-us), a second kind of ciliate. *Trachelius* looks like a round, blobby rhinoceros and is about twice the size of *Campanella*. *Trachelius* uses its cilia not for feeding but to help it swim around. *Campanella* has no eyes so it doesn't notice *Trachelius* swimming nearby, but no worries. There is plenty of room in the pond for both of them.

Or maybe not.

As soon as it bumps into *Campanella*, *Trachelius* attacks. It stretches its mouth wide and begins slurping up its prey like an algae-filled ice-cream cone. *Campanella* puts up a spirited defense. It contracts, or shrinks, to throw off the attacker. It tries to dodge to the side, but tethered in place by its stalk, it can't get away. In moments, *Trachelius* completely swallows its ciliate cousin whole. It's a disaster for *Campanella* but just another day in the ciliate-eat-ciliate world.

CAMPANELLA MEANS "BELL" IN BOTH LATIN AND ITALIAN—A REFERENCE TO THE PROTOZOAN'S BELL-LIKE SHAPE.

PREDATORY PROTOZOA

Ciliates such as *Campanella* and *Trachelius* belong to a vast group of microscopic organisms called protozoa. At least thirty to fifty thousand different kinds of protozoa live on our planet—and probably a lot more. They come in a huge variety of bizarre, often beautiful, shapes. Most consist of only a single cell, and many have cilia that they use to feed or swim through their environments.

Are Protozoa Animals?

Scientists have had a lot of trouble figuring out how to classify protozoa. Some protozoa seem more like plants, while others seem more like animals. Scientists refer to predatory ciliates as "animal-like."

Protozoa make their livings in a variety of ways. A few get their energy from the sun. Others graze on bacteria. Many are parasites. They feed off the tissues of other animals or live inside the bodies of other animals and steal food from them. Some of the most interesting protozoa are predators that gobble up their microscopic neighbors. They are among the tiniest predators on the planet— but not all of them look like *Trachelius*.

PROTOZOA ARE POLYPHYLETIC. THIS MEANS THAT DIFFERENT GROUPS OF PROTOZOA EVOLVED FROM DIFFERENT ANCESTORS AND THAT NOT ALL PROTOZOA ARE CLOSELY RELATED.

MICRORAPTORS

You've probably heard of amoebas—slow-moving protozoa that change shape and engulf their food by wrapping their blobby bodies around it. But did you

A tiny pinch of soil can contain as many as *fifteen thousand* amoebas. A small volume of ocean water might contain millions of protozoa!

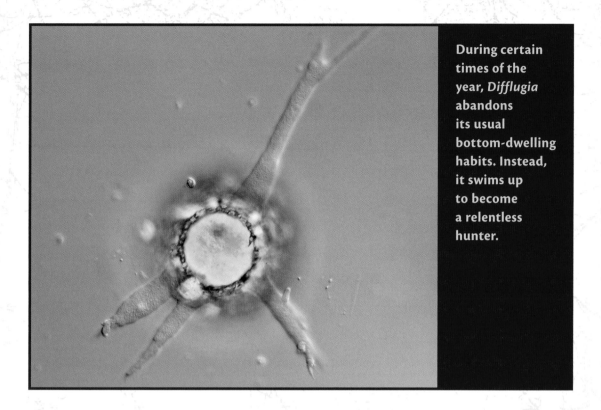

During certain times of the year, *Difflugia* abandons its usual bottom-dwelling habits. Instead, it swims up to become a relentless hunter.

know that some amoebas live inside of shells? Scientists called them testate, or shelled, amoebas.

Testate amoebas usually live on the bottom of a lake or pond, or attached to an underwater plant. There, they feed on tiny algae and other particles of food. Recently, though, Chinese scientists noticed something unusual about a testate amoeba called *Difflugia*. *Difflugia* spends part of the year on lake bottoms, but during some seasons, it swims freely in open water. When that happens, it switches its feeding mode. Instead of eating small particles, it becomes a relentless hunter!

Difflugia has a special fondness for one kind of tiny animal, a rotifer. The rotifer lives inside of a jellylike tube that protects it from predators—usually!

Let's Split!

Many protozoa reproduce by mating just as much larger animals do, but many others reproduce by dividing their bodies into two separate individuals. This kind of reproduction is called fission.

Rotifers are about the same size as many protozoa and also have cilia but are in their own phylum of animals, the Rotifera. While many protozoa consist of only a single cell, a rotifer's body is complex, containing advanced internal organs and thousands of different cells. About fifteen hundred species of rotifers live on Earth.

When *Difflugia* encounters a rotifer, it sends out two long blobby fingers as if measuring the size and position of its prey. Next, it moves to the bottom of the rotifer's jelly tube and manages to open a hole in it. The rotifer contracts, trying to shrink or get away, but trapped inside its jelly tube, it has nowhere to go. *Difflugia* seizes the foot of the rotifer and, in the words of one scientist, sucks it in "like a piece of spaghetti."

LITTLE CRITTERS, BIG IMPACTS

Even though protozoa are tiny, they play vital roles on our planet. Some cause disease, but most perform positive tasks in our environment. Without protozoa, we and most other kinds of living things would not be able to live on Earth. Protozoa are some of Earth's most important *decomposers*. They can break down, process, and recycle waste products in our environment. Protozoa also devour bacteria, keeping their numbers under control. Photosynthetic protozoa act like plants and use the sun's energy to make their own food—and the oxygen we breathe. Protozoa are also a key food source for other tiny animals. And what about predatory protozoa such as *Trachelius* and *Difflugia*? They help control the numbers of small critters such as rotifers—and other protozoa!

CHAPTER 3
PREDACEOUS PTEROPODS

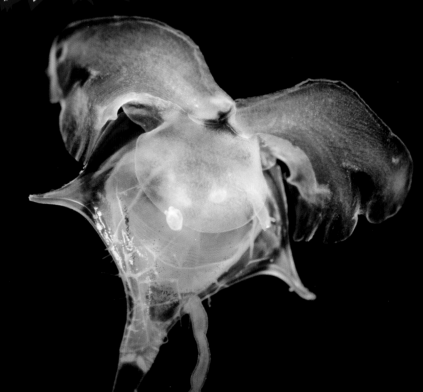

A sea butterfly called a three-spine cavoline

Out in the ocean, several hundred feet deep, a beautiful little creature called a sea butterfly swims through the water. The animal has a shell and two appendages, like graceful wings, that propel it forward. It casts a mucus net in front of it to capture food particles, and when the net fills up, the sea butterfly ingests it and casts a new one. As it is feeding, another small, gorgeous creature approaches. This second animal—a sea angel—looks a lot like the sea butterfly except that it has no shell. Instead of peacefully "fishing" for food, however, the sea angel suddenly attacks the sea butterfly! Using tiny hooks and suckers, it latches onto its prey, yanks it out of its shell, and swallows it. Now empty, the sea butterfly's shell sinks slowly toward the ocean floor.

KILLER COUSINS

Both the sea butterfly and the sea angel are tiny swimming snails called pteropods (TARE-oh-pawdz). Scientists have identified more than 120 species of pteropods. They range in size from microscopic to about an inch (2.5 cm) long. The foot of these snails has evolved into beautiful wings that pteropods use to swim gracefully through the sea. Even though pteropods can swim, they are considered to be planktonic. They are swept from place to place by ocean currents.

Pteropods belong to two different groups. One group is the shelled pteropods, or sea butterflies. Sea butterflies have tiny shells, and they're vegetarians—sort of. They collect food with nets or globs of mucus. This mucus catches tiny plants, or phytoplankton, but it also catches food called *marine snow*. Marine snow is made up of poop, skin, mucus, plant material, and dead body parts of other animals. You probably wouldn't order a marine snow sandwich, but shelled pteropods love the stuff. By eating marine snow, sea butterflies play an important role in recycling the ocean's food energy.

PTEROPOD MEANS "WINGED FOOT" IN LATIN.

The second group of pteropods—sea angels—has no shells. Marine snow? Sea angels wouldn't touch the stuff. Instead, they prey on—you guessed it—the first group of pteropods!

A rain of slowly falling marine snow supports a whole community of ocean life including sea butterflies, eel larvae, and vampire squids.

Amphipod Abduction

In the Antarctic, tiny shrimplike animals called amphipods—which are related to "pill bugs"—catch pteropods and carry them around on their backs. Why? Because for at least some ocean animals, pteropods taste bad—and that deters hungry fish looking for an amphipod snack!

No one is quite sure how sea angels find their shelled relatives. Once they do, they grasp their prey with tiny curved hooks and tentacles that are normally tucked inside their heads. Then they make a meal out of their unfortunate cousins.

And you thought your family reunions were awkward!

POTATO CHIPS OF THE SEA

Besides recycling marine snow, pteropods play a vital role in the ocean's food web. Most live in the upper 500 feet (152 m) or so of the ocean, and there, they become food for fishes, squid, seabirds, and even whales. So many animals eat pteropods that they are sometimes called the potato chips of the sea.

A sea angel gets its name from the two short "wings" that help it glide through the ocean.

Unfortunately, climate change puts pteropods at risk. How? Sea butterflies build their shells out of calcium carbonate, a hard substance that they extract from the ocean. Humans have been releasing millions of tons of carbon dioxide gas, or CO_2, into Earth's atmosphere by burning fossil fuels such as coal and gasoline. When that CO_2 is absorbed by our oceans, it makes the waters more acidic. The calcium carbonate dissolves so that animals can

Ptera Ooze

When pteropods die, their shells sink to the bottom of the ocean and dissolve like a wet piece of chalk. Over thousands of years, so many pteropod shells have collected that they help form a sediment of ooze across some parts of the ocean floor.

no longer use it. Already, ocean waters have turned acidic enough to eat away at the shells of sea butterflies. The sea butterflies fight back by adding extra layers of calcium to thicken their shells, but this likely takes a toll on the animals, and no one is sure how well sea butterflies will survive if we cannot reduce CO_2 levels in the atmosphere.

If sea butterflies disappear, their shell-less cousins the sea angels will too. Together, these events will impact the many other animals that eat pteropods. Pteropods, as much as any other animals, demonstrate how interconnected all ocean species are. They show us how important it is to take better care of our planet by switching to solar power, wind power, and other nonpolluting energy sources.

Pteropods Up and Down

Many kinds of pteropods move up and down in the ocean every day. At night they rise closer to the surface to feed. During the day, they sink back into the darker—and safer—depths. Many other marine species also perform these daily vertical migrations.

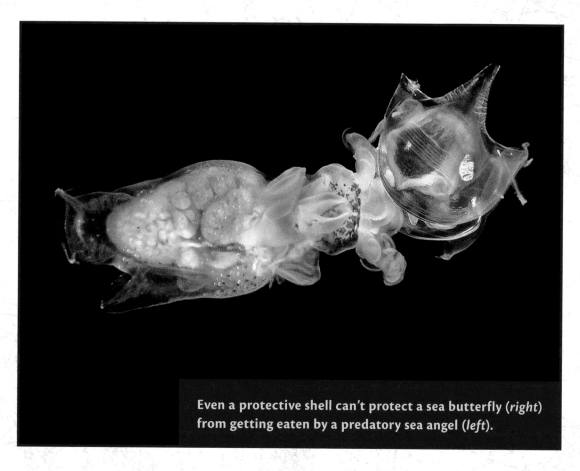

Even a protective shell can't protect a sea butterfly (*right*) from getting eaten by a predatory sea angel (*left*).

CHAPTER 4
FATAL FLATWORMS

A typical marine turbellarian flatworm

About twenty years ago on the Pacific island of Guam, marine biologist Raphael Ritson-Williams found a new kind of ocean worm no one had ever seen before. He dropped the worm into a container full of seawater and kept looking for other animals. Soon he came across a beautiful shelled snail called a cowrie (COW-ree) and, without thinking about it, dropped the cowrie into the same container as the worm. When he returned a little while later, he was shocked. The cowrie shell was still there, but the snail *inside* had disappeared. Instead, it formed a large lump

TURBE TERRORS

Ritson-William's worm belonged to a remarkable group of animals called turbellarian flatworms, or turbellarians (ter-buh-LAIR-ee-unz). At least six thousand species of these worms live on Earth, and they can be found in the ocean, on land, and in lakes and rivers. A few land turbellarians are "giants," growing to more than a foot (0.3 m) long, but the vast majority are less than half an inch (1.3 cm), including many microscopic species. Turbellarians can feed on dead things, but most are predators. They have been known to devour snails, earthworms, oysters, stinging animals called hydroids, barnacles, copepods, amphipods, and—surprise!—other turbellarians. How do they do it?

The sturdy shells of cowries look like little fortresses, but they are no match for the poison of some turbellarian worms.

TURBELLARIAN TOOLS OF THE TRADE

Turbellarians capture their prey in a variety of ways. Their mouths are on the undersides of their bodies and can be stretched extremely wide. Like many other animals, turbellarians also come equipped with a *pharynx* (FARE-inks). This tube is in the throat area behind the mouth. In many flatworms, the pharynx is especially muscular and can be stuck out like a little vacuum-cleaner attachment.

When many turbellarians encounter a prey animal, they wrap their bodies around it, entangling and pinning their victim. Turbellarians have numerous mucus glands in and below their skin, and the worms may use their slime to help trap an animal too. Once the prey is pinned, a flatworm may swallow it whole (if it's small enough) or the flatworm may insert its pharynx into its victim. The pharynx releases chemicals called enzymes that begin

Flatworm Families

Scientists used to consider all turbellarian flatworms to be closely related, but further study has revealed that turbellarian flatworms, like protozoa, are polyphyletic. Different groups of the worms evolved from different ancestors.

digesting the prey before it is swallowed. As the tissues of the victim begin breaking down into smaller chunks, the flatworm simply "vacuums" them up.

But for many victims, it gets worse.

TURBELLARIAN TTX

When Ritson-Williams found the cowrie snail inside his newly discovered worm, he wondered how the worm had managed to kill the snail and get it out of its shell. Cowries have muscles that hold them tightly inside their shells, and not even a human can pull one out. So how did the flatworm do it? By conducting several experiments with different flatworms, Ritson-Williams found that the worms have a secret weapon—tetrodotoxin (TET-roe-doe-TOCK-sin), or TTX.

Most turbellarians live in water, but some "giants" live on land. A few have become pests after being accidentally transported to places they don't belong and gobbling up native worms and other animals.

Tetrodotoxin is a potent poison. It can be found in many animals, from salamanders and puffer fish to blue-ringed octopuses and at least a few chaetognaths. TTX can help an animal defend itself, but it can also help it paralyze its prey. Ritson-Williams could not see his flatworms actually release their TTX, but the amount of poison in each worm's pharynx was a lot lower after feeding than it was before. From this, the scientist concluded that the worms released a deadly cloud of tetrodotoxin that a snail absorbed into its body when it breathed. The poison paralyzed the snail, preventing it from contracting, or tightening, its muscles. When the snail relaxed, the worm used its pharynx to yank the cowrie from its shell and eat it.

Mystery Toxin

Although tetrodotoxin appears in many different animals, it's a mystery where exactly it comes from. Scientists believe that bacteria may actually manufacture the poison, so some animals might get TTX from bacteria living inside of them. Other animals, however, may have to get their tetrodotoxin by eating TTX-containing prey. More scientific research is needed to completely solve this mystery.

FAR-REACHING FLATWORMS

Scientists still have a lot to learn about turbellarian flatworms. Very few of them have been studied and probably hundreds—or even thousands—have not even been discovered. Turbellarian flatworms, though, play huge roles in our world. In almost every kind of habitat, they are some of the world's most important micropredators, devouring countless kinds of creatures. Many turbellarians are also important study animals, helping scientists make biological and medical discoveries. One group of freshwater turbellarians called planarians is especially famous. Why? Because if you cut a planarian into pieces, a complete living animal will regrow from each piece! This makes them especially interesting to scientists and doctors who work on medical transplants and regrowing lost or damaged organs such as kidneys.

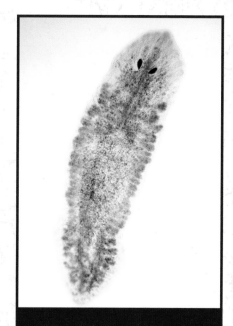

Planarian flatworms are important laboratory animals, helping scientists study many topics including the ability of animals to regrow body parts!

With their voracious appetites, it's no surprise that some turbellarians are pests. Land turbellarians have hitchhiked from one country to another in nursery plants and potting soil. In France, scientists discovered that at least five species of turbellarians have invaded their country—including two that can grow to more than 18 inches (45 cm) long! Scientists worry that in France and many other countries, these flatworms are gobbling up native earthworms and other small animals that are important to local ecosystems. And they aren't the only little killers causing big problems.

CHAPTER 5
CARNIVOROUS COMBS

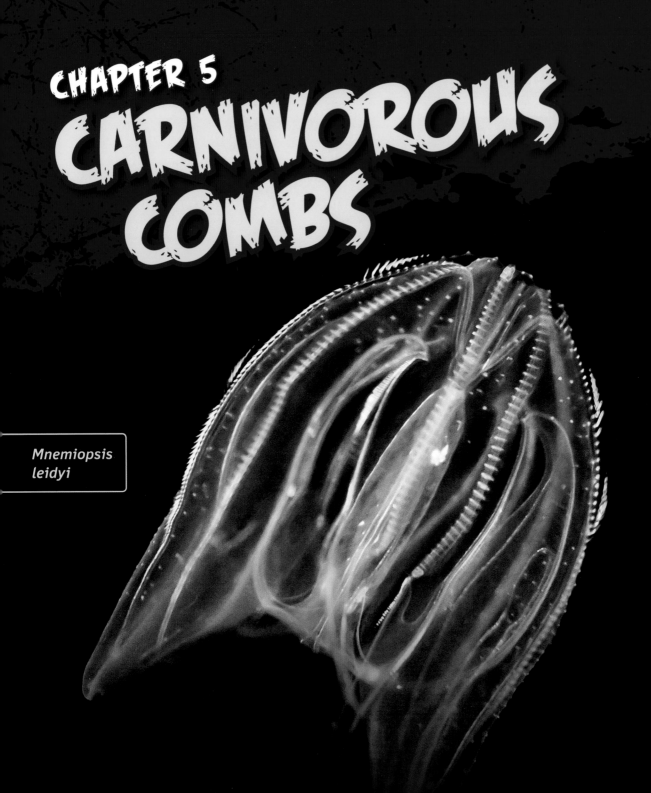

Mnemiopsis
leidyi

I n the 1980s, the Black Sea was already in trouble. Overfishing and pollution had reduced the numbers of fish, putting many fishermen out of work. Then a hacky-sack-sized jelly animal showed up.

The animal was called *Mnemiopsis leidyi* (NEH-mee-OP-sis LAY-dee-eye), and it probably arrived in a ship's ballast water. Empty ships pump ballast water into their hulls to make them more stable during a voyage. At the end of the voyage, they usually dump the water at their new location. Unfortunately, the water often carries harmful hitchhikers with it. Sometime around 1982 a ship dumped one or more *Mnemiopsis* into the Black Sea.

It was a disaster.

Within several years, the Black Sea ecosystem had almost entirely collapsed. Fishing boats could barely catch any fish. Other animals all across the food web disappeared. Why? Because *Mnemiopsis* had gobbled up the fish larvae, fish eggs, and tiny zooplankton that the Black Sea ecosystem depended on.

ZOOPLANKTON IS ANOTHER WORD FOR PLANKTONIC ANIMALS. PHYTOPLANKTON REFERS TO PLANTS, OR ALGAE, THAT ARE PLANKTONIC.

DEADLY BEAUTY

Mnemiopsis is a kind of comb jelly, or ctenophore (TEE-no-four). About two hundred species of ctenophores live in the world's oceans and saltwater seas, and they are some of Earth's most beautiful— and hungriest—predators. Most are bioluminescent. They glow a spectacular blue or green color when bumped or attacked.

"Giant" ctenophores can reach more than 4 feet (1.3 m) long, but most range from smaller than a pea to just a few inches long. At first glance, ctenophores look like jellyfish. Many have gelatinous, see-through bodies. They also feed on many of the same tiny creatures as jellyfish do. Ctenophores, though, are a separate group of animals.

Ctenophores get their name *comb jellies* from eight rows of combs on their bodies. These combs are filled with clusters of cilia that beat in waves or ripples up and down the combs. As the cilia move, they row the

Ctenophores, or comb jellies, are some of Earth's most beautiful and important ocean animals.

ctenophores slowly through the water. But don't let this relaxed swimming fool you. Some comb jellies can eat many times their body weights in a single day. They eat so much that they can make a significant dent in the zooplankton and eggs of other animals around them.

POPULOUS PREDATORS

While jellyfish usually catch their prey with long tentacles loaded with stinging cells, ctenophores have several different ways to grab a meal. One large group of ctenophores comes armed with only two tentacles. Instead of stinging cells, these tentacles have sticky cells called *colloblasts*. The ctenophores hang suspended in the water or move very slowly and spread their tentacles—almost like a spider web—snagging whatever small animals they encounter.

Mnemiopsis belongs to a second group known as lobate ctenophores. Instead of two long tentacles, they have lobes around their mouths. Little structures called auricles, which have beating cilia, slowly sweep water between these lobes. The cilia move the water so slowly that a prey animal doesn't try to escape until it has almost reached the ctenophore's mouth. By then it is too late. Tiny tentacles on the lobes capture the panicked prey, and the ctenophore devours it.

Mnemiopsis, however, has its own ctenophore to worry about.

STAYING STILL AND WAITING FOR YOUR PREY TO SHOW UP IS CALLED A SIT-AND-WAIT METHOD OF HUNTING. THIS STRATEGY IS USED BY MANY KINDS OF CTENOPHORES THAT HAVE TENTACLES.

Luminous Appetites

Many ctenophores eat bioluminescent prey, but since ctenophores are transparent, they risk attracting their own predators if their dinners are glowing inside them. Some ctenophores solve this problem by having stomachs lined with light-blocking pigments.

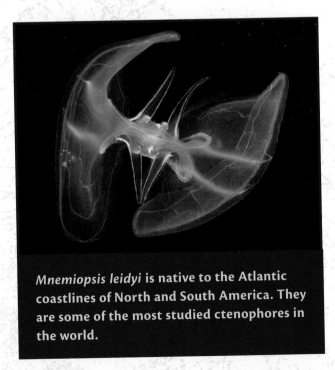

Mnemiopsis leidyi is native to the Atlantic coastlines of North and South America. They are some of the most studied ctenophores in the world.

SECOND WAVE

More than a decade after the 1982 invasion of *Mnemiopsis*, another kind of ctenophore accidentally got dumped into the Black Sea. Like *Mnemiopsis*, *Beroe ovata* is a ruthless killer. Unlike *Mnemiopsis*, its prey is other ctenophores. *Beroe* lacks long tentacles or lobes. When it encounters a *Mnemiopsis*, *Beroe* simply swallows it whole!

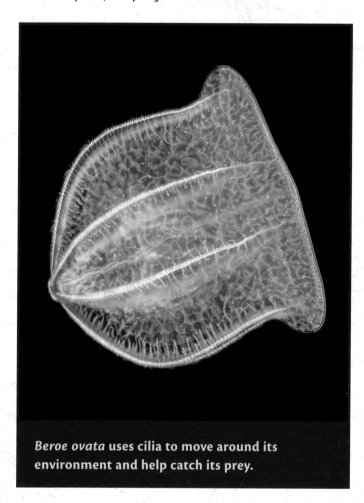

Beroe ovata uses cilia to move around its environment and help catch its prey.

Beroe's arrival in the Black Sea was dramatic. Within a year or two, it reduced *Mnemiopsis* numbers so much that native populations of fish and zooplankton began to recover. Since then, *Mnemiopsis* and *Beroe* also have spread to the Mediterranean and Baltic Seas. Their impacts have been less severe than in the Black Sea, but scientists are watching them closely. These and other ctenophores leave no doubt that these beautiful killers can have a huge impact on ocean life—and that it is in our best interest to keep each species where it belongs.

Crawling Combs

Most ctenophores swim freely, but several species crawl along the sea bottom or attach themselves to animals on the seafloor. These species lack combs but have short clusters of tentacles for catching prey. Divers often mistake these brightly colored creatures for sea slugs or worms.

CHAPTER 6
LETHAL LADYBIRD BEETLES

A typical ladybird beetle eating an aphid

On June 4, 2019, California weather experts were confused. Skies were clear and no rain was forecast, but a huge, mysterious cloud had appeared on weather radar maps. The cloud seemed to float about a mile (1.6 km) above the ground and stretch up to 80 miles (129 km) across. What's more, the mysterious blob was moving. What was that thing?

What insects lack in size, they can make up for in numbers—especially when they form large swarms!

To find out, one of the meteorologists telephoned a contact in the path of the cloud. It turned out that the cloud wasn't rain or even dust. It was a massive swarm of millions—make that *billions*—of ladybird beetles!

WORLD'S CUTEST KILLERS

Ladybird beetles, or simply ladybirds, are some of the most well-known insects on Earth. People often call them ladybugs, but these critters aren't bugs. Bugs belong to the insect order Hemiptera (hem-IP-ter-uh), which includes animals such as leafhoppers and cicadas. Ladybird beetles are true beetles in the family Coccinellidae (KOK-sih-NEL-ih-dee). Anyone who has ever spent time outdoors has seen ladybird beetles walking along grass stems or perched on flowers. Their small size and brightly colored wing covers could easily earn them the title of World's Cutest Insects.

THE WORD COCCINELLIDAE COMES FROM A LATIN WORD MEANING "CLAD IN SCARLET." MANY LADYBIRD BEETLES ARE RED.

Scientists have identified about six thousand different species, or kinds, of ladybird beetles. They come in a rainbow of colors, and many sport stylish polka dots. Ladybirds can feed on plants, fungus, or pollen, but don't be fooled.

Most are killers.

Predators Beware!

A ladybird's flashy colors aren't for show. They warn other predators: "I taste bad, so don't even try it." Ladybird beetles are loaded with poisonous chemicals. When attacked, many ladybirds release toxic fluids from their joints to drive off predators. This is called "reflex bleeding."

KILLER TIMES TWO

Ladybird beetles have two active phases of life. Once they hatch from eggs, they enter their *larval phase*. During this phase, ladybird beetles look like stubby little caterpillars or mini alligators. The larvae are often black or gray with splotchy orange or yellow spots. Without wings, they must crawl from one place to another.

IN INSECTS, THE TRANSFORMATION FROM EGG TO LARVA TO PUPA TO ADULT IS CALLED METAMORPHOSIS.

Over the next few weeks, a larva goes through several stages, or *instars*, during which it sheds its outer layer, or *cuticle*, so that it can grow larger. After

Like their parents, ladybird beetle larvae devour hundreds of aphids and other tiny plant-sucking insects.

Farmers all over the world have imported ladybird beetles to fight aphids, scale insects, and other plant pests. Unfortunately, some of these ladybird beetles have become pests themselves.

four or five instars, it becomes a *pupa*. It forms a hard case around itself and undergoes a remarkable transformation from a stubby little larva into the beautiful winged creature that we all recognize.

Unlike butterflies and many other insects, the larvae and adults of many ladybird beetles feed on the same food. Their prey? Mostly aphids and scale insects. These animals live on plants and have piercing mouthparts that they poke into plant stems and leaves. They suck the juices from these plants and, in large numbers, can kill or weaken the plants they live on.

How Hungry?

Reports of how many aphids an adult ladybird beetle can eat vary from twenty-five to several hundred aphids *per day*. A typical larva eats a total of at least two to three hundred aphids before it turns into an adult.

Ladybird beetles take advantage of this situation. Female ladybird beetles lay their eggs on plants loaded with prey insects. After hatching, the larvae crawl up and down the stems of their host plant, hunting their prey by smell and touch. Whenever they encounter an aphid or scale insect, they kill it with their scissorlike jaws, or *mandibles*. Larger larvae can consume an aphid or scale insect whole. Smaller larvae inject digestive enzymes into the animal and suck out the juices.

MANY LADYBIRD BEETLES ARE CANNIBALS, EATING THE EGGS, LARVAE, AND ADULTS OF THEIR OWN SPECIES.

Mmmm—aphid smoothie!

WINGED WARRIORS

At close range, adult ladybird beetles can probably locate prey by sight. Both larvae and adult ladybirds also come equipped with sensitive antennae. The antennae are loaded with cells called *sensilla* that allow the beetles to detect their prey by smell and touch. Scientists still have a lot to learn about the beetles' sense of smell, but several studies show that some ladybird beetles can definitely smell aphids from short distances. One big advantage for adults is that when pickings are slim, they can fly to another plant to search for food. This ability has made ladybird beetles especially useful to farmers and gardeners since the beetles move around and protect a large number of plants.

In the 1880s, California was one of the world's most important sources of oranges, lemons, and other citrus fruits. By 1888 the orchards were under siege by the cottony-cushion scale. In just months, this pest insect devastated California's citrus industry. Farmers pulled out and burned their dead citrus trees. They tried poisoning the scale insects with deadly cyanide. Nothing worked and the scale continued to spread.

Ladybird Freeloaders

Many kinds of ladybirds are famous for gathering in huge masses to hibernate—usually in mountainous areas. Some choose to gather in people's homes. The insects can release a nasty odor and often have to be removed. Pest control experts may also seal up cracks and holes and spray certain chemicals to keep ladybird beetles out.

Then a scientist named C. V. (Charles Valentine) Riley imported five hundred ladybird beetles from Australia, along with a kind of parasitic fly. His team started breeding and releasing these insects throughout citrus orchards in California. Within a couple of years, the cottony-cushion scale had all but disappeared.

This use of ladybird beetles may be the first successful use of *biological control* to conquer a harmful pest. Since then, dozens of ladybird species have been imported to farming areas around the world. This may not always be a good thing. While the ladybird beetles have helped farmers, the insects also may be harming native ladybird beetles by competing with them for food.

Stinky Wine

Wine producers aren't crazy about ladybirds and their toxic smells. When the beetles feed on crushed grapes and those grapes end up in wine, it can ruin the entire batch. In one experiment, as few as three beetles in 2.2 pounds (1 kg) of crushed grapes caused wine drinkers to turn up their noses at the wine that was produced.

CHAPTER 7
SWARMING SPIDERS

Anelosimus eximius spiders swarming a trapped dragonfly

It is an overcast morning in the Amazon. A yellow butterfly flutters through the warm, humid air searching for a flowering plant to feed on. It heads toward a group of promising bushes that may have some nectar-filled flowers to sip. Suddenly, without warning, the butterfly hits an invisible, sticky wall. The insect struggles to escape, but instead of freeing itself, it attracts the attention of several tiny red spiders. As the butterfly flaps harder, more spiders appear until two dozen surround the insect

Each spider is only about the size of a thumbtack and would have a hard time tackling the butterfly on its own. These spiders, though, work together. In a flash, several spiders dart in to bite the butterfly. They inject their venom and begin wrapping the insect in spider silk. The butterfly keeps flapping, but its wingbeats grow weaker and weaker. Within minutes, it is dead.

Victorious, the spiders haul their prey to a nearby nest where hundreds of hungry mouths wait to be fed.

SPIDER SOCIETIES

No one knows how many different spiders inhabit our planet. Scientists have named about forty thousand species, but at least twice that many may be waiting to be discovered and described. What no one doubts is that spiders are Earth's ultimate little killers. With a few plant-eating exceptions, spiders are predators.

Females Rule

Most social spiders are females, and not surprisingly, they do most of the care of spiderlings and handling of prey. In a study of *Anelosimus eximius*, scientists found that male spiders made up only between 5 percent and 22 percent of a colony's population.

The large webs of social spiders are familiar sights in parts of Africa and South America.

Live Fast, Get Eaten

Social spiders don't live long. Some species in Africa live about a year. Those in South America live only a few months. Younger spiders often get a head start in life by eating their aunts and mothers!

Like most other little killers, the vast majority of spiders hunt or trap prey on their own, without help from any other spiders. Around the globe, however, several very special kinds of spiders have developed spider societies. These tiny spiders build shared nests, help take care of one another's young and, most importantly, cooperate to trap and subdue prey. Scientists call them social spiders.

TREMENDOUS TRAPS

Although they are very small, social spiders often are easy to spot—if you're in the right part of the world. You'll be walking through a South American rain forest and suddenly come upon a massive web up to 20 or 30 feet (6 to 9 m) tall and wide. This silk fortress can be home to thousands of spiders—all of the same species.

Working together allows social spiders to capture more—and larger—prey, and also to cooperate in raising their young.

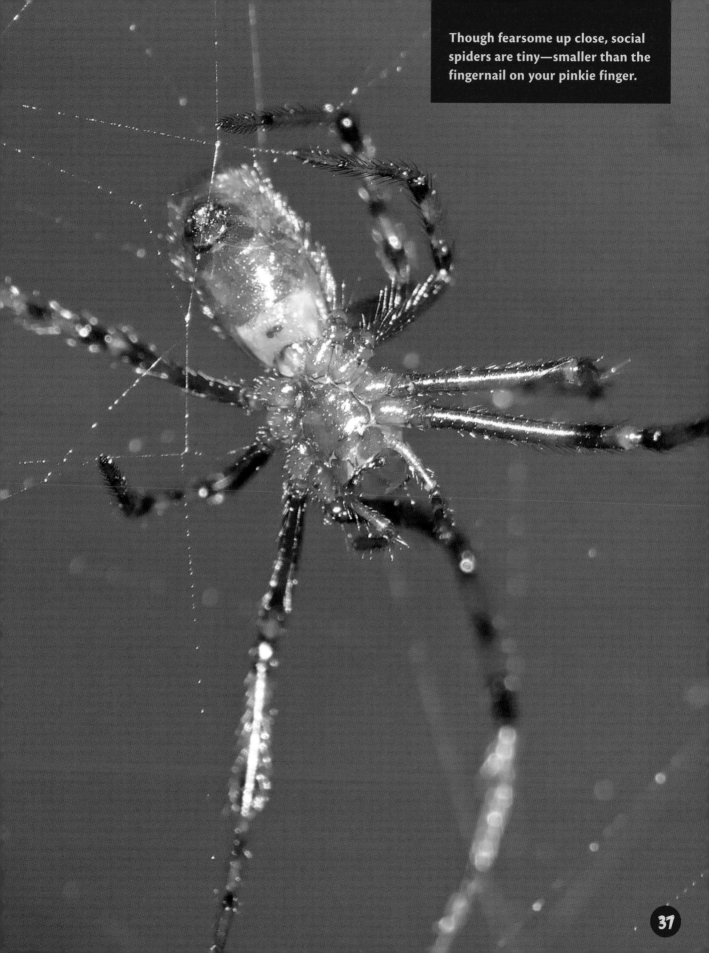

Though fearsome up close, social spiders are tiny—smaller than the fingernail on your pinkie finger.

Web Designers

The colonies of South American social spiders have two distinct parts. The spiders spin capture webs to intercept and capture prey. Within—or at the base of—the capture webs, the spiders build nests of silk, leaves, and other materials. These nests are where the spiders take shelter and raise their young.

Their web is a marvel of engineering. The South American spider *Anelosimus eximius*, for instance, places vertical strands of silk, like guitar strings, at the top of its nests. Flying insects run into these strands and, while a lucky few may escape, most are doomed. They either get stuck in the strands or fall down into a sticky trap below. Unfortunately, the more a victim struggles, the more vibrations it sends throughout the social spiders' web. The more vibrations, the more spiders come to investigate. Small flies may attract only one or two spiders. Large grasshoppers or cockroaches might draw dozens of assailants.

The question is, Why work together?

Grasshoppers and other larger insects often fall prey to the "teamwork" of social spiders.

SOCIAL ADVANTAGES

Scientists have come up with several reasons why it might be an advantage for social spiders to cooperate:

- Larger webs allow the spiders to capture larger prey that provide more food for the entire colony.
- In places where high winds or heavy rains damage webs, multiple workers can make repairs more quickly.
- Larger webs and more spiders might make it harder for enemies to attack them.
- Having many spiders to care for eggs and the young might improve the survival odds of the next generation.

That doesn't mean that the life of a social spider is easy. A tropical storm or flood can easily wipe out an entire colony. If a colony grows too big for the amount of nearby prey, the colony may starve to death. Social spiders also have enemies. Certain species of solitary spiders have adapted to living within social spider webs and steal their prey. Parasitic wasps lay their eggs in the bodies of living social spiders, and when their larvae hatch, they eat the spiders alive!

Despite these hardships, species of social spiders have evolved many different times and in many different places. That tells us that working together can be useful. In fact, it's not surprising that other little killers also have evolved to work together . . .

Spider Overpopulation

While South American spider colonies *can* have thousands of members, scientists have found that colonies seem to survive better with only a few hundred. Why? There may be several reasons, but one study found that when colonies grow too large, the amount of prey captured can't keep up with the number of mouths to feed. That makes it more difficult for every spider to get enough food.

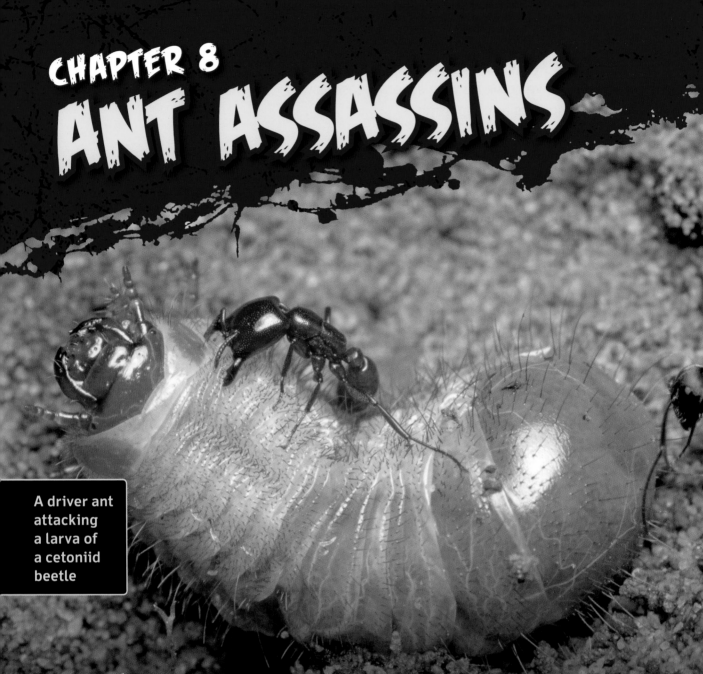

CHAPTER 8
ANT ASSASSINS

A driver ant
attacking
a larva of
a cetoniid
beetle

A mass of ants leaves its underground nest and heads into the forest. The ants come in several sizes but are all the same species, and as more and more of them head out, their column begins to resemble a thick, writhing rope. This living rope is hundreds of ants wide, and it contains thousands, then tens of thousands, then *millions* of ants. The column consists mostly of small worker ants and is protected by larger soldier ants that position themselves with their jaws spread wide at the edges of the column. Eventually, the column begins to fan out into a wide front or wave, creeping forward at about 1 foot (0.3 m) per minute.

Soon it begins encountering its prey. As the ants move forward, they surprise unsuspecting grasshoppers, spiders, beetles, slugs, butterflies—and even rats and other small mammals too slow to get out of their way.

When one ant discovers prey, it releases a chemical alarm signal and within seconds, other ants join in the attack. With deadly efficiency, they pounce on their prey, overwhelming their victims with powerful jaws and sheer numbers. Even before some of the animals have died, the ants begin chopping them up and carrying them back to the nest. For their victims, the attack is a disaster. For the attackers, it is just another day in the life of one of Earth's most remarkable little killers, the driver ant.

AS THEY WALK, ANTS LEAVE BEHIND A CHEMICAL TRAIL THAT OTHER ANTS CAN FOLLOW. ANTS FOLLOW THESE TRAILS TO LEAD THEM TO FOOD, A NEW NEST, OR WHEREVER ELSE THEY MAY BE NEEDED.

Driver ants form unstoppable columns as they swarm out to look for food.

Ant Cycle

Like many other insects, driver ants go through a four-part life cycle. The egg hatches into a larva that looks like a little caterpillar or worm. After eating and growing *a lot*, the larva enters a resting stage called a pupa. The pupa may be inside of a cocoon or just a hardened skin (exoskeleton), but in this stage, it grows legs and other adult parts. Finally, it bursts out of its cocoon or skin as an adult.

MILLIONS OF MOUTHS

Driver ants are a type of army ant. At least fifty different species are spread across Africa and Asia, but the heart of their range lies in the rain forests of the Congo and West Africa.

These ants share many similarities to the more famous army ants of Central and South America. Driver ants live in huge colonies and spread through the forest attacking any animal they can find. They have a nomadic lifestyle, frequently moving from their current home base to another location. Like many of Central and South America's army ants, driver ants are blind. They detect their prey—and one another—by smell, taste, and touch with their highly sensitive antennae. As they walk, individual ants leave behind chemical scents that help direct other ants where to go.

Driver ants do have important differences from their American counterparts. Driver ants often stay in one place longer and can dig complex galleries and chambers up to 12 feet (3.7 m) belowground. Driver ants are only about the length of your fingernail, but their queens are some of the world's largest known ants, growing more than 2 inches (5 cm) long. These queens are the ultimate egg-laying machines, pumping out *one to two million eggs per month*. It's no surprise that a single colony of driver ants can number twenty-two million ants—many times larger than America's army ants! Feeding so many mouths is a colossal, often brutal, task.

ANT ATTACK

Every day, the driver ants head out in a new direction. Some driver ants specialize in eating earthworms, but most devour any animal in their paths. They sweep the forest clean of almost all other invertebrates—insects, spiders, worms, and other animals without backbones. They attack small

mammals and even climb trees, where they can kill nests full of baby birds. Driver ants provide a valuable service to people by eating dead cows and other carrion that they encounter.

Driver ants can sting but rarely do. Instead, they tear apart their prey. Driver ant soldiers are the ultimate meat heads. Their heads are filled mostly with muscles that operate their incredibly powerful mandibles, or jaws. For their size, the power of their jaws has been compared to the force of a car-crushing machine, and like other ants, they can carry loads heavier than their own body weights. As some ants surge forward to attack, others ferry food back to the nest, where the queen and millions of juvenile and worker ants wait to be fed.

KEYSTONE KILLERS

As devastating as they are as predators, driver ants greatly benefit their forest habitat. By clearing out the other small animals from an area, the ants keep any one species from becoming too abundant or problematic. By preying on plant-eating insects, the ants may help protect a variety of plant species too. Numerous kinds of birds depend on driver ant columns. When the ants flush or stir up insects and other invertebrates, the birds pounce and snag themselves a meal.

A number of flies, beetles, and other tiny animals have evolved to take advantage of the ant colonies. Their bodies or odors trick the driver ants into thinking that they also are ants. One group of flies steals prey and eats the larvae of driver ants. Rove beetles have evolved to look and behave like ants of many different species. They are known to eat the ants' young.

Deadly Trio

Not counting the queen and large winged males that mate with her, adult driver ants come in three distinct sizes. Soldier ants are the largest, measuring almost 0.5 inches (13 mm). They defend the colony and help chop up especially challenging prey. Medium workers do most of the killing, butchering, and prey transport. Small workers, only 0.13 inches (3 mm) long, provide many different services for the colony, including attacking and transporting prey, cleaning the nest, and moving eggs, pupae, and larvae.

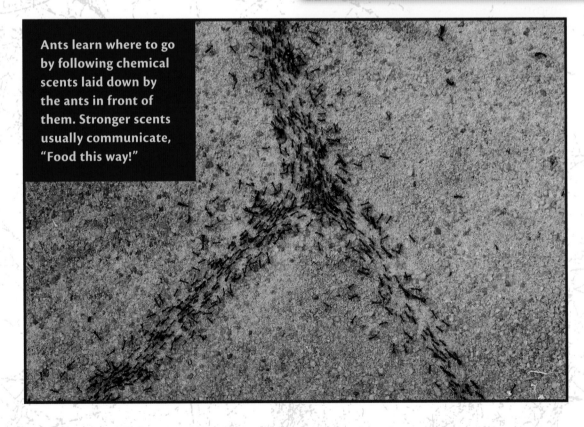

Ants learn where to go by following chemical scents laid down by the ants in front of them. Stronger scents usually communicate, "Food this way!"

Driver Road Trips

Scientists aren't exactly sure what triggers driver ants to move to a new location, but food scarcity and egg-laying cycles may have something to do with it. One study showed that attacks by mammalian predators also caused driver ant colonies to move immediately. The ants may build a new nest only a couple of football fields away from a previous location, but driver ant workers carefully prepare for the move by clearing paths and digging new tunnels and chambers. Then they make multiple trips transporting the eggs, pupae, and larvae. Meanwhile, the giant queen also begins her slow crawl to her new home. Each move usually takes about three days to complete, and ants may return to previous nest locations again and again.

Chimpanzees frequently prey on driver ants. The primates insert sticks into driver ant nests or columns. Then they remove the sticks and slurp off any ants that have glommed onto them. Scientists refer to this as "ant dipping," and it is a fascinating use of a tool by a nonhuman animal.

Whether they are predators or prey, driver ants play such an important role in tropical forests and other ecosystems that scientists refer to them as *keystone species*—essential for an ecosystem to stay healthy. Without its driver ants, a tropical forest or savanna becomes a much different, poorer place. It is one more reason for humans to learn about and protect *all* animal species—even the smallest.

CHAPTER 9
PROTECTING TINY PREDATORS

The amphibian-killing fungus *Batrachochytrium dendrobatidis*

You've met some of Earth's tiniest predators. Hopefully, you've realized that these predators are some of the *most important* predators too. When they land in the wrong place, they can cause big problems. However, when they are doing what they're supposed to—and in the place they're supposed to—little killers help keep our planet in balance. They control pests and diseases. They help keep our waters and soils healthy. Some can even help protect endangered species.

AMPHIBIAN PROBLEMS

Beginning in at least the 1970s, a group of fungi began attacking at least seven hundred species of frogs and salamanders. The fungi showed up on every continent except Antarctica—and with devastating effects. Almost overnight, scientists began noticing dozens of frog species going extinct, while populations of many other amphibians dropped to critical levels. Scientists scrambled both to figure out what was going on and to save species, and they especially wanted to know why the fungi proved so lethal to some amphibian species and not to others.

Since then, scientists have learned that many factors affect how deadly a fungus is. These include temperature and pollution, as well as which particular strain of the fungus is attacking a particular amphibian. One group of scientists made a remarkable discovery. In the Pyrenees mountain range of Europe, they found that the presence of predatory protozoa dramatically reduced the deadliness of a fungus called *Batrachochytrium dendrobatidis*, or "Bd" for short. How?

To spread and multiply, the Bd fungus releases spores that look like microscopic pollywogs. These spores have tails and swim around until they find a frog or salamander to attack. If an amphibian gets infected by enough spores, it grows sick and dies.

Scientists discovered, however, that several kinds of protozoa gobble up fungal spores as if they were ramen noodles. In waters without the protozoa, frogs got severe infections and many died. In other waters, the protozoa ate so many spores that frogs had no infections or very mild ones. These frogs survived.

MICRO UNDERSTANDING AND PROTECTION

As the fungus-frog example shows, we ignore small predators at our own peril. Not only can they cause problems, but they can protect us and many other species. Unfortunately, we still know very little about most little killers. As a society, we need to support scientists so that we can learn more about these predators. We need to take steps both to protect little killers and make sure they don't spread to places where they don't belong. These are some steps we can take:

- **Reduce the use of pesticides on farms and in yards.** Pesticides often kill predators such as ladybird beetles and spiders, letting pest animals get out of hand. Pesticides also harm people directly by causing diseases and poisoning our food and water.

Deforestation devastates wildlife, including driver ants and many other small predators.

- **Reduce the use of artificial fertilizers**. Fertilizers often get washed into rivers and lakes, fueling blooms of undesirable algae and other organisms. This upsets the balance of entire ecosystems and can eliminate many beneficial micropredators.
- **Protect natural habitats.** Protecting forests, rivers, and wetlands ensures that small predators have healthy, safe places to live. Forest destruction in West and central Africa, for instance, eliminates colonies of driver ants, leading to the disappearance of birds and other species that depend on them.
- **Stop the spread of invasive species**. As certain flatworms and ctenophores prove, the wrong critter in the wrong place can lead to disaster. Not enough governments do a good job of inspecting and regulating the flow of organisms from one place to another.

Signs such as this help remind people to clean their boats and equipment before moving to other waterways.

Government intervention needs to improve if we are to protect our planet's wealth of little predators.

- **Halt climate change.** Probably our biggest challenge—and the most important—is to reverse the dramatic rise in Earth's temperatures. This rise is mainly caused by burning coal, oil, and natural gas for energy. When burned, these fuels release enormous quantities of carbon dioxide into our atmosphere, leading to a steady increase in the world's temperatures. This already is having catastrophic impacts on Earth's environment and the millions of plant and animal species that live here. A short list of these impacts includes increased and more extreme floods, fires, and droughts; rising sea levels; the disappearance of forests; and the acidification of the oceans. If we want to save pteropods and thousands of other tiny killers, we need to make a worldwide effort to bring temperatures back down.

No matter your age or situation, everyone can help. We can save energy by turning off lights and driving our cars less. We can make sure we don't buy exotic pets and plants unless they have been certified as pest-free. We can get involved in local projects to protect species and improve the environment. We can urge our government representatives to work toward the long-term health of our planet and vote against actions that are harmful or shortsighted. Mostly, we can educate our friends and parents about tiny predators by explaining how important they are and how we can protect them. A healthy natural environment is important for both the smallest animals and the largest, like us. Why not dig out a microscope or a magnifying glass and show other people a few tiny predators up close and personal? If more people know how closely linked we all are to the natural environment, then maybe more of us will take action to protect it. Even if you can't see little killers, your efforts will make our planet a better place to live for them—and for us.

Studying tiny predators can be a fascinating adventure. On a short walk, you might find several little creatures who are hunting their next meal.

Author's Note and Acknowledgments

I have been enchanted by little killers ever since watching a ctenophore under a microscope in Professor Mimi Koehl's invertebrate zoology class at UC Berkeley. As a kid I had heard of ctenophores—and even gotten into a ctenophore fight with my dad one night in the waters of Woods Hole, Massachusetts. Not until I watched a ctenophore close up, though, did I have any idea how magnificent these critters were. The way its cilia beat in rhythmic waves and the animal's two tentacles floated gracefully in the water almost took my breath away.

Ever since, I have been aware how underappreciated Earth's smallest animals are—especially its predators. Wolves, sharks, tigers, and other large predators get the, ahem, lion's share of attention in books, films, and nature programs. Earth's little predators? Well, they pretty much get ignored. This book is an attempt to correct that situation. I hope that it's shown you that Earth's micropredators are just as incredible and important as larger predator "movie stars."

I'd like to thank my editors, Carol Hinz and Jesseca Fusco, for sharing my enthusiasm for this subject and working with me to make this the ultimate book about tiny predators. I also could not have written *Little Killers* without the generous time and effort of many scientists and other experts. A special shout-out to Dr. Steven Haddock (mbari.org; jellywatch.org) of the Monterey Bay Aquarium Research Institute and UC Santa Cruz for reviewing the entire manuscript, as well as for his special expertise on chaetognaths, ctenophores, and pteropods. Other scientists went out of their way to make suggestions on specific chapters and ensure they were as accurate as possible. A huge thanks to them:

Dr. Jim Driver, University of Montana, for "Microscopic Meat Eaters";

Raphael Ritson-Williams, California Academy of Sciences, San Francisco (raphswall.com), for "Fatal Flatworms";

Jen Marangelo, Glenn Marangelo, and Karen Weaver, Missoula Butterfly House and Insectarium (missoulabutterflyhouse.org), for "Lethal Ladybird Beetles";

Dr. Ambika Kamath, University of Colorado, Boulder (ambikamath. wordpress.com), for "Social Spiders"; and

Professor John Longino, University of Utah, for "Ant Assassins."

Glossary

auricles: projections or knobs surrounding the mouth of a ctenophore, and lined with cilia that direct water currents and food toward the mouth

biological control: control or elimination of a pest by using predators, diseases, or other living things to keep it in check

cilia: tiny hairlike structures that are used for locomotion or feeding in certain kinds of living things

ciliates: a large group of protozoa that are defined by the presence of cilia on their bodies

Coccinellidae: the family of beetles containing ladybird beetles

colloblasts: sticky cells on the tentacles of ctenophores that help the animals catch and hold prey

copepods: a varied and widespread group of small aquatic crustaceans related to shrimp, crabs, and lobsters

cuticle: a hard or waxy covering of an insect and certain other animals and plants

enzyme: a chemical that helps a certain action or process take place, such as digestion, but doesn't get altered or used up itself

instars: different stages in the development of larval animals

larvae: the immature stage or stages of insects and many other kinds of animals. Often larvae look and behave much differently from adults.

mandibles: the crushing or slicing mouthparts found in insects, crustaceans, and other animals; also the jaws of mammals and upper and lower parts of a bird's beak

marine snow: a "rain" of mucus, fecal matter, and other organic material that sinks slowly down through the ocean and provides food for many ocean animals

metamorphosis: how a larval animal transforms into an adult, including butterflies, crabs, starfish, and many other animals

microscopic: too small to see with the naked eye

pharynx: a muscular tube connecting the mouth and stomach of many animals. In some, it is modified to serve as a probe or to deliver poison or digestive enzymes.

phytoplankton: plants that are planktonic

plankton: any living thing that is transported mainly by water currents

polyphyletic: a group of living things having more than one line of ancestors

protozoa: a large group of mostly single-celled organisms including amoebas and ciliates

pupa: the stage of an animal between its larval and adult stages while it is undergoing metamorphosis. It is usually enclosed in a protective case.

regenerate: in living things, to regrow a body part

voracious: requiring a lot of something (such as food) to be satisfied

Source Notes

15   Bo-Ping Han et al., "Carnivory and Active Hunting by the Planktonic Testate Amoeba *Difflugia tuberspinifera*," *Hydrobiologia* 596, no 1 (2008): 200.

Selected Bibliography

A major difference between "megapredators" and their smaller counterparts is that often very little is known about smaller predators. Textbooks might have general information about protozoa or a particular flatworm used for medical research, but most little killers still await thorough—or any—scientific study. As a result, I combed through scientific research papers to choose and learn about most of the animals featured in this book. Videos also proved enlightening and, in the case of *Trachelius*, provided me with an organism to focus on. To make sure that I got my facts correct, I took the extra step of asking more than half a dozen experts to review what I'd written. They provided invaluable suggestions and corrections for the book. Below are just a few of the dozens of references that I drew upon to write *Little Killers*.

Chaetognaths & Copepods
Ball, Eldon E., and David J. Miller. "Phylogeny: The Continuing Classificatory Conundrum of Chaetognaths." *Current Biology* 15, no. 16 (2006): R593–596.

Protozoans
Han, Bo-Ping, Tian Wang, Qiu-Qi Lin, and Henri J. Dumont. "Carnivory and Active Hunting by the Planktonic Testate Amoeba *Difflugia tuberspinifera*." *Hydrobiologia* 596 (2008): 197–201.

Van Egmond, Wim. "*Trachelius* Ciliate Feeding on *Campanella* Ciliate." 2015 Small World in Motion Competition, Nikon Small World. Accessed September 9, 2021. https://www.nikonsmallworld.com/galleries/2015-small-world-in-motion-competition /trachelius-ciliate-feeding-on-a-campanella-ciliate.

Pteropods
Burridge, Alice K., Erica Goetze, Deborah Wall-Palmer, Serena L. Le Double, Jef Huisman, and Katja T. C. A. Peijnenburg. "Diversity and Abundance of Pteropods and Heteropods along a Latitudinal Gradient across the Atlantic Ocean." *Progress in Oceanography* 158 (November 2017): 213–223. https://www.sciencedirect.com/science /article/pii/S0079661116300040.

Turbellarians

Ritson-Williams, Raphael, Mari Yotsu-Yamashita, and Valerie J. Paul. "Ecological Functions of Tetrodotoxin in a Deadly Polyclad Flatworm." *PNAS* 103, no. 9 (February 28, 2006): 3176–3179. https://www.pnas.org/content/103/9/3176.

Ctenophores

Haddock, Steven H. D. "Comparative Feeding Behavior of Planktonic Ctenophores." *Integrative and Comparative Biology* 47, no. 6 (December 2007): 847–853. https://doi.org/10.1093/icb/icm088.

Ladybird Beetles

Cosgrove, Jaclyn. "High-Flying Ladybug Swarm Shows Up on National Weather Service Radar." *Los Angeles Times*, June 4, 2019. https://www.latimes.com/local/lanow/la-me-ln-ladybugs-on-radar-20190604-story.html.

Majerus, M. E. N. *A Natural History of Ladybird Beetles*. Edited by Helen E. Roy and Peter M. J. Brown. Cambridge: Cambridge University Press, 2016.

Social Spiders

Goldman, Jason G. "Meet the Spiders That Have Formed Armies 50,000 Strong." BBC, January 22, 2016. http://www.bbc.com/earth/story/20160122-meet-the-spiders-that-have-formed-armies-50000-strong.

Driver Ants

Lucas, Neil, dir. *Natural World*. "Ant Attack." Season 24, episode 13. Aired January 25, 2006, on BBC Earth. Clip of episode available as YouTube video, 3:58. Posted by BBC Earth, August 29, 2019. https://www.youtube.com/watch?v=ZglirAfRvWg.

Protecting Tiny Predators

Frazer, Jennifer. "Frog-Killing Fungus Meets Its Match in Tiny Predators." *Scientific American* (blog), April 28, 2014. https://blogs.scientificamerican.com/artful-amoeba/frog-killing-fungus-meets-its-match-in-tiny-predators/.

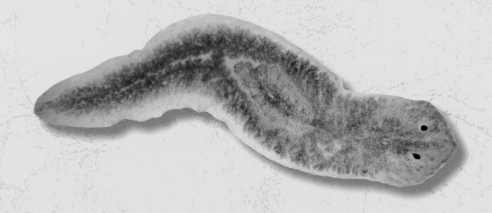

For Further Investigation

Very few books about tiny predators have been written for nonscientists. The books below give a taste of certain little killers, but a rich "micro" trove of information also can be found on the following videos listed. Enjoy!

Books

Bishop, Nic. *Spiders*. New York: Scholastic, 2007.
This award-winning book by photographer Nic Bishop offers incredible up-close photos of spiders, including some of them in action. It will change how you view these tiny, beneficial predators.

Hallmén, John, and Lars-Åke Janzon. *Bugs Up Close: A Magnified Look at the Incredible World of Insects*. New York: Skyhorse, 2020.
One of the problems with small predators is that we don't get to see them up close. This book offers remarkable up-close photos of insects, including many that are predatory.

Jenkins, Steve, and Robin Page. *Tiny Monsters*. Boston: Houghton Mifflin Harcourt, 2020.
In this gorgeous picture book, the authors introduce a host of tiny creatures—including some predators—that usually go unnoticed in the world. They also give great size comparisons between the illustrations and the actual sizes of the animals.

Montgomery, Heather. *Little Monsters of the Ocean*. Minneapolis: Millbrook Press, 2019.
Take a look at the often predatory larvae of ocean animals as they go through metamorphosis.

Pringle, Laurence. *Spiders! Strange and Wonderful*. Honesdale, PA: Boyds Mills, 2017.
In this elegant, beautifully illustrated book, a veteran science writer shares astonishing facts and basic biology of one of Earth's most important group of predators.

Stewart, Melissa. *Deadliest Animals*. Washington, DC: National Geographic, 2011.
This is a fascinating look at a wide variety of predators both big and small.

Websites & Videos

"Discovering Marine Invertebrates with Karen Osborn." YouTube video. 29:16. Posted by Smithsonian's Museum of Natural History, March 18, 2016. https://www.youtube.com/watch?v=dqxdiLSwa0w.
This is a fun interview with a scientist who studies many tiny killers in the ocean. It includes information on how scientists learn about these critters.

Monterey Bay Aquarium Research Institute
https://www.youtube.com/channel/UCFXww6CrLAHhyZQCDnJ2g2A
A collection of fascinating videos on a wide array of ocean animals, including many small predators.

Raph's Wall
http://www.raphswall.com/chemical-ecology.html
Check out an awesome video of a flatworm attacking a snail. You will be amazed!

"Researching Chytridiomycosis—First Successful Treatment for Frogs." YouTube video. 5:41. Posted by Understanding Animal Research, May 23, 2016. https://www.youtube.com/watch?v=5X7juDb6oKM.
This video explains the scientific efforts to combat the fungi that are killing amphibians.

"Social Spiders Spin Massive Nest." YouTube video. 3:28. Posted by Nature on PBS, April 14, 2015. https://www.youtube.com/watch?v=td09PIjzoiQ.
This is a wonderful video of social spiders at work.

Index

Photo Acknowledgments

Image credits: Nature Picture Library/Alamy Stock Photo, p. 1; irin-k/Shutterstock.com, p. 2 (top); Ernie Cooper/ Shutterstock.com, p. 2 (bottom); Choksawatdikorn/Shutterstock.com, pp. 4, 23; © Solvin Zankl/NPL/Minden Pictures, p. 5; Freebird7977/Shutterstock.com, p. 8; micro_photo/iStock/Getty Images, p. 10; M. I. Walker/Science Source, p. 11; Panther Media GmbH/Alamy Stock Photo, p. 12; blickwinkel/Alamy Stock Photo, p. 13; blickwinkel/F. Fox/Alamy Stock Photo, p. 14; Solvin Zankl/Alamy Stock Photo, p. 16; Courtesy of the National Oceanic and Atmospheric Administration Central Library Photo Collection, pp. 17, 18 (bottom); David Fleetham/Alamy Stock Photo, p. 18 (top); Blue Planet Archive/Alamy Stock Photo, p. 19; WaterFrame/Alamy Stock Photo, pp. 20, 24; cbimages/Alamy Stock Photo, p. 21; FLPA/Alamy Stock Photo, p. 22; Jeff Milisen/Alamy Stock Photo, p. 25; imageBROKER/Alamy Stock Photo, pp. 26, 27; Denis Crawford/Alamy Stock Photo, p. 28; Anton Starikov/Alamy Stock Photo, p. 29; Henrik_L/iStock/Getty Images, p. 30; Gilles/Wikimedia Commons (CC BY-SA 2.0), p. 31; Premaphotos/Alamy Stock Photo, p. 34; Jason Wrench/Getty Images, p. 35; BIOSPHOTO/Alamy Stock Photo, p. 36; Courtesy of the author, p. 38; Avalon.red/Alamy Stock Photo, p. 40; Simon Colmer/Alamy Stock Photo, p. 41; H Lansdown/Alamy Stock Photo, p. 43; Joe Blossom/Alamy Stock Photo, p. 44; Dr Alex Hyatt, CSIRO/Wikimedia Commons (CC BY 3.0), p. 46; Dudarev Mikhail/Shutterstock.com, p. 48 (top); Mark Boulton/Alamy Stock Photo, p. 48 (bottom); MILATAS/Getty Images, p. 49; Ger Bosma Photos/ Shutterstock.com, p. 55.

Cover: Nature Picture Library/Alamy Stock Photo (ant); irin-k/Shutterstock.com (ladybug); Ernie Cooper/Shutterstock. com (flatworm); Premaphotos/Alamy Stock Photo (spiders); Textures and backgrounds/Shutterstock.com (background); nicemonkey/Shutterstock.com (background).